DATE DUE	
DEC 0 6 2010		

The Urbana Free Library

To renew materials call
217-367-4057

Math in the Real World

How Crime
Fighters Use Math

By Sheri L. Arroyo

Math Curriculum Consultant: Rhea A. Stewart, M.A.,
Specialist in Mathematics, Science,
and Technology Education

**CHELSEA
CLUBHOUSE**
An Imprint of Chelsea House Publishers

8/10   26.00

Math in the Real World: How Crime Fighters Use Math

Chelsea Clubhouse
An imprint of Chelsea House Publishers
132 West 31st Street
New York NY 10001

Library of Congress Cataloging-in-Publication Data
Arroyo, Sheri L.
        Math in the real world: how crime fighters use math / by Sheri L. Arroyo;
            math curriculum consultant, Rhea A. Stewart.
            p. cm. — (Math in the real world)
        Includes index.
        ISBN 978-1-60413-602-9
        1. Criminal investigation—Mathematics—Juvenile literature. 2. Criminology—Mathematics—
        Juvenile literature. 3. Criminology—Vocational guidance—Juvenile literature. I. Stewart, Rhea A.
        II. Title. III. Series.
        HV8073.8.A77 2010
        363.2501'51—dc22   2009023330

Chelsea Clubhouse books are available at special discounts when purchased in bulk quantities
for businesses, associations, institutions, or sales promotions. Please call our Special Sales Department
in New York at (212) 967-8800 or (800) 322-8755.

You can find Chelsea Clubhouse on the World Wide Web at http://www.chelseahouse.com

Developed for Chelsea House by RJF Publishing LLC (www.RJFpublishing.com)
Text and cover design by Tammy West/Westgraphix LLC
Illustrations by Spectrum Creative Inc.
Photo research by Edward A. Thomas
Index by Nila Glikin

Photo Credits: 4, 10, 16, 18, 26: AP/Wide World Photos; 8: John Boykin/Photolibrary;
12: © Mikael Karlsson/Alamy; 14, 15, 24: iStockphoto; 20: David Jones/PA Wire URN:5843877
(Press Association via AP Images); 22: © HEINZ-PETER BADER/Reuters/Corbis.

Printed and bound in the United States of America

Bang RJF 10 9 8 7 6 5 4 3 2 1

This book is printed on acid-free paper.

All links and Web addresses were checked and verified to be correct at the time of publication.
Because of the dynamic nature of the Web, some addresses and links may have changed since
publication and may no longer be valid.

Table of Contents

Answers and helpful hints for the You Do the Math
activities are in the Answer Key.

Words that are defined in the Glossary are
in **bold** type the first time they appear in the text.

Using Math to Fight Crime

Every day, crime fighters work hard to keep people safe. They search for clues and evidence to help find and stop people who break laws. Some crime fighters work for local police departments. Others work for the Federal Bureau of Investigation, also known as the FBI.

To find criminals, crime fighters study handwriting samples, tire tracks, and footprints. They stop **graffiti**, find **forged** paintings, and break secret codes. Dive teams look for clues underwater, and "cyber" detectives work to stop computer crimes. For all of these crime fighters, math is an important part of their work.

Computer Crime

Many crimes today involve computers. Sometimes computers are stolen. Sometimes people create harmful programs called viruses that can wipe out information or cause computers to

Crime fighters look for clues at the scene of a crime.

4

be unable to process information correctly. Often, viruses are spread over the Internet. Sometimes people who work for a company use a company computer in ways that they shouldn't. People angry at the company they work for may even try to destroy important information kept in the company's computers.

Recently, the FBI wanted to know how many companies have been the victims of crimes that involved computers. The FBI did a **survey** to find out. The bar graph below shows what 100 companies told the FBI.

How Many Computer Crimes?

Use the bar graph that shows what the FBI learned about computer crimes to answer these questions.

1. How many times did a company report having a laptop computer stolen?

2. What problem was reported more than any other?

3. How many fewer times was music illegally downloaded than information was destroyed?

4. How many computer problems did the companies have altogether?

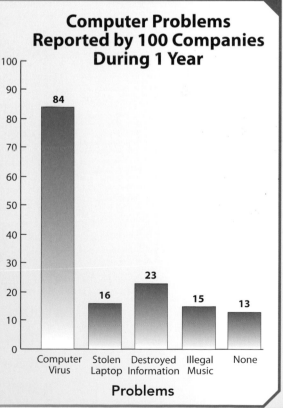

Computer Problems Reported by 100 Companies During 1 Year

Number of Reports

Problem	Number
Computer Virus	84
Stolen Laptop	16
Destroyed Information	23
Illegal Music	15
None	13

Problems

CSI: Crime Scene Investigation

When a crime happens, an **investigator** is called to the scene. As soon as she arrives, she does a careful check of the entire area. She decides what specialists (people with specific training) will be needed. For example, should she bring in people with training in studying handwriting, tire tracks, fingerprints, or footprints? Next, the investigator makes a plan for collecting and recording the evidence. Then, she begins to make a sketch of what she sees.

Sketching and Measuring

The sketch, or drawing, of the crime scene is a clear record of what the investigator sees before anything is touched or moved. She uses graph paper to draw an outer **perimeter** of the scene. (The perimeter is the distance around the outside.) Then, she adds things that are inside the perimeter. If the crime scene is a room, for example, she adds furniture and other objects found within the room to the grid. She also measures the distances between objects.

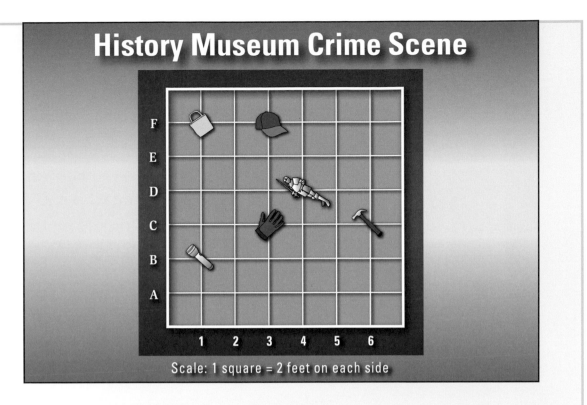

History Museum Crime Scene

Scale: 1 square = 2 feet on each side

The investigator also photographs the scene. She takes separate photographs of all of the objects. Detectives will use her sketch and photographs as they work on the case.

You Do the Math

Reading a Crime Scene Sketch

Now you be the detective! The shield from a knight's suit of armor has been stolen from the history museum. Use the crime scene sketch above to answer the questions. Points on a grid are called coordinates. When you name coordinates, you say the location on the horizontal axis first, then the location on the vertical axis. For example, in the sketch above, the glove is at coordinates (3, C).

1. Name the coordinates that tell where the flashlight is located.

2. Name the coordinates for the hammer.

3. What object is at (4, D)?

4. Where did the detectives find the baseball hat? Name the coordinates.

Are You Telling the Truth?

C rime fighters use lie detectors, or polygraph machines, to try to figure out if someone is telling the truth. Detectives want to know if people accused of a crime who say they didn't do it are telling the truth or not. A polygraph is an instrument that measures changes in a person's body, such as changes in how fast your heart is beating or how fast you are breathing. These changes can provide helpful information.

How Lie Detectors Work

For a polygraph test, several wires and other devices are connected to the person who is taking the test. An examiner asks questions, and the devices send information to a computer about the person's breathing rate, heart rate, and sweat on the fingertips. When the person is answering certain questions, does he breathe more quickly? Does his heart beat more rapidly? Does he sweat

The man at left is taking a polygraph test at a police station. The computer records information about such things as his breathing and heart rate when he answers each question.

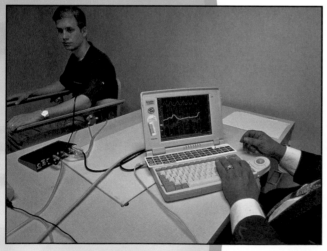

more? These kinds of reactions can be signs that the person is not telling the truth.

Sometimes it is hard to tell, though. Polygraphs record a person's reactions to questions, but they do not necessarily prove that a person is lying. The polygraph results have to be studied by the examiner, who is trained to review polygraph tests and make conclusions about the data gathered. The examiner writes a report about whether the person who was tested told the truth or not in answering each question. The more training and experience examiners have, the more likely it is that their conclusions will be **accurate**.

You Do the Math

Which Examiner Is Most Often Right?

The table shows the results of some polygraph tests given by four examiners. Each examiner gave ten polygraphs. Look at the results to see how accurate each examiner has been. For each examiner, write a fraction that represents the number of correct tests (the numerator) divided by the total number of tests given (the denominator). Rank the examiners from most accurate to least accurate. (Remember: When the denominators are the same, the largest fraction is the one with the greatest numerator.)

Polygraph Tests Given by Four Examiners		
Examiner	Total Number of Tests Given	Number of Correct Tests
A	10	6
B	10	8
C	10	5
D	10	4

Tracking a Criminal: Shoeprints

Shoeprints left at an outdoor crime scene can give an investigator a lot of information. He can **estimate** how tall the person is who made the print. He can estimate how much the person weighs.

An investigator measures the length of the shoeprint, the depth of the shoeprint, and the stride—how far apart the prints are. A shorter person will usually have smaller feet (the length of the shoeprint won't be very long) and a shorter stride. A taller person will usually have bigger feet (the length of the print will be longer) and a longer stride. Also, the more a person weighs, the deeper the shoeprint will be.

Investigators carefully search for shoeprints at the scene of a crime.

Other Clues

Detectives can get other clues from shoeprints that also can help solve the crime. Shoes sold by different companies have specific patterns on the soles. Investigators can make **casts** of the shoeprints by filling the prints with a soft substance. When the substance gets hard, the casts can be removed and studied. This may help detectives figure out where the shoes were bought. By checking that store's customer records, they may find the criminal.

You Do the Math

Analyzing Shoeprints

Four people (Suspects A, B, C, and D) are suspected of committing crimes.

Suspect A is tall and thin.

Suspect B is medium height and heavy.

Suspect C is short and heavy.

Suspect D is short and thin.

The table below gives information about a shoeprint made by each suspect. Which suspect most likely made each shoeprint? Look at the measurements to help you decide.

Shoeprints Made by Four Suspects			
Shoeprint	Shoeprint Length (in inches)	Stride Length (in inches)	Depth of Print
1	7	24	shallow
2	13	48	shallow
3	10	36	deep
4	8	24	deep

Evidence in Writing

When a detective is trying to figure out if two papers were written by the same person, she may ask a handwriting expert to analyze, or study, samples of the handwriting on the papers. A person's handwriting can be as individual as his fingerprints.

When a person signs another person's name to a document, such as a check or a credit card slip or a legal paper, it is called forgery. Forgery is a crime. Handwriting analysis is used to detect forgery. Handwriting analysis can also be used to figure out who wrote a document. Perhaps someone received a letter saying that a harmful action would take place, but the letter was not signed. A handwriting expert might be able to figure out who wrote the letter.

A handwriting expert uses a computer to compare two handwriting samples.

Types of Analysis

When a detective works on a forgery case, she first gets a handwriting sample from the suspect. Then, she asks an expert to study the handwriting. The expert looks to see where the writer starts to make each letter and looks at how the letters are slanted. The expert also measures how much space is left between letters and words. And the expert notices how large the letters are and how different letters are connected together. All of these features can help the expert to figure out whether the handwriting sample and the writing on the forged document were done by the same person.

Forgery Cases

A detective worked on 100 forgery cases during a year. The circle graph shows types of forgery cases the detective worked on. In each case, the name signed on a document was a forgery. Use the graph to answer the questions.

1. What type of case did the detective work on more than any other?

2. How many fewer cases involved legal paper forgery than bank account forgery?

3. How many forgery cases involved either credit cards or bank accounts?

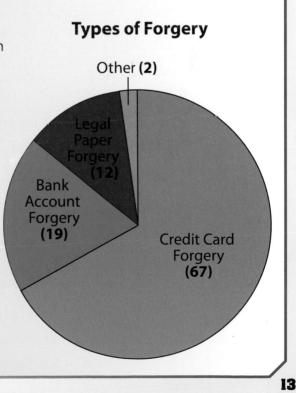

Types of Forgery

Other (2)

Legal Paper Forgery (12)

Bank Account Forgery (19)

Credit Card Forgery (67)

Slow Down!

Highway police may have a way to figure out if a person is driving too fast—even if a police officer never saw the person's car. Drivers must pay a toll (a fee) to drive on certain highways. On some of these toll roads, drivers may receive piece of paper (a ticket) at a toll booth that tells what time they entered the highway and where they entered. As they leave (or exit) the road, they give the ticket to the toll booth operator and pay the fee. The time and place they leave is also stamped on the ticket. Sometimes a computer system at the toll booths records at what time and where a driver entered and exited a highway.

When drivers pay tolls on a highway, the times at which they enter and exit the road may be recorded.

Going Too Fast

If drivers get to their exit too quickly, they may be given a speeding ticket. How did the police know a driver was speeding? First, a computer **calculates** how many miles the person traveled and how much time it took him to drive those miles. Then, it calculates how fast he was driving (the driver's speed) by dividing the miles traveled by the time it took to drive that distance. If the driver's speed was faster than the speed limit, the person may get a ticket.

You Do the Math

Driving on Toll Roads

Four drivers traveled on a road. Each person drove for one hour. For each driver, the start mileage and the end mileage show where, along the road, each driver got on and off. The **difference** between the start mileage and the end mileage for each driver is the number of miles traveled. First, figure out how many miles each driver traveled in an hour. If the speed limit is 55 miles per hour, which drivers were going too fast and could get a speeding ticket?

Distances Traveled on a Highway		
Driver	**Start Mileage**	**End Mileage**
A	55	125
B	37	91
C	16	65
D	49	109

Tracking Graffiti

When people paint or write without permission on public places such as walls, bridges, or sidewalks, what they paint or write is called graffiti. Graffiti damages property and costs a lot of money to clean up. Creating graffiti is against the law, and crime fighters work very hard to stop it from happening.

Police keep track of when and where graffiti has been found. They take photographs of what was painted or written and compare it to other cases to see if the same person may be responsible. They

Workers in the city of Phoenix, Arizona, clean graffiti off the wall of a building.

also record the dates, times, and exact locations where graffiti was found. They use this information to try to **predict** when and where the **vandals** might strike next, so police officers can be ready to catch them.

The Cost of Graffiti

What does it cost to clean up graffiti? Every year, many cities spend between $1 and $3 for each person who lives in that community on graffiti removal. The money adds up. In 2006, the city of Denver, Colorado, spent $1 million to clean up graffiti. Houston, Texas, spent $2.2 million, and Chicago, Illinois, spent $6.5 million.

Cleaning Up Graffiti

The towns of Maplewood, Sycamore, and Elmhurst spend a great deal of money each year cleaning up graffiti. The table shows how many people live in each town and how much is spent per person yearly on graffiti removal. How much money does each town spend in total each year? Which town spends the most money? Is it the town with the largest number of people?

Money Spent to Clean up Graffiti		
Town	**Population**	**Money Spent per Person on Graffiti Removal**
Maplewood	30,000	$2.60
Sycamore	45,000	$1.25
Elmhurst	75,000	$1.00

Is This Painting the Real Thing?

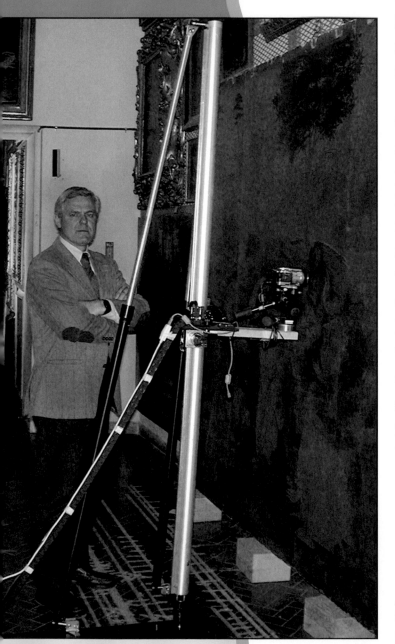

An art expert stands next to equipment used to scan paintings.

Paintings by famous artists, such as Vincent Van Gogh, are world treasures. They hang in museums, and many people see them every day.

Sometimes people try to copy a famous artist's style. They pretend that a painting they made was really created by the famous artist and try to sell it for a great deal of money. Art historians and experts use different ways to decide if a painting is **authentic**—that is, if it was actually painted by a particular artist.

An Artist's "Mathematical Signature"

Experts who are **mathematicians** are working with museums to identify an artist's style. First, they **digitally scan** a painting. Then, they divide the scan into smaller sections. Each section is a square that has sides about 2 inches long. Mathematicians look for patterns in the lines of the artist's brush strokes. How long are the brush strokes? How many brush strokes are there? This becomes the artist's "mathematical signature." Mathematicians can compare the brush strokes of another painting to one they are certain was painted by a famous artist. Then, they can tell if the other painting is authentic or not.

You Do the Math

How Many Works of Art?

1. City Art Museum scanned its collection of paintings and found that it has 127 authentic paintings. Museum workers also found that the museum has 47 other paintings that are not authentic. What is the total number of paintings that the museum has?

2. City Art Museum also examined its collection of statues to see if they are authentic. It found that they all are. Another museum loaned City 28 more statues to put on display for a few months. Now, City Art Museum has 59 statues on display. How many statues did City have to start with?

3. State Art Museum is scanning its 78 paintings. Famous Art Museum has 43 more paintings than State Art Museum has. How many paintings does Famous Art Museum have?

Diving for Evidence

When crime fighters need to find evidence that is on the bottom of a lake or river or even in the ocean, what do they do? They call for specially trained dive teams. Many police departments have dive teams. The FBI also has special dive teams known as USERTs—Underwater Search and Evidence Response Teams.

The evidence divers look for might be something a criminal had stolen but now doesn't want to get caught with. Or perhaps the evidence is a tool that a criminal used to break into a house and has now gotten rid of so that it can't be checked for fingerprints.

A police dive team searches for evidence that may be underwater in this river.

Tools and Technology

Crime fighting dive teams are underwater experts. They know how to use special underwater equipment. They need special equipment because it can be dark and cold underwater. Also, the water may be cloudy and dirty, making things difficult to see. Side scan **sonar** is one tool that helps divers find things in cloudy water or mud. Divers also use underwater metal detectors.

When divers find evidence, they measure out a grid and mark the location of everything they see on the grid. They also take photographs of the evidence. Then, they carefully collect the evidence. Detectives use the information from the grid as well as the evidence in their investigation.

Underwater Search

A dive team has measured out 2 underwater search sites that are next to each other where the divers will look for evidence and plot it on their grid maps.

Underwater Search Sites
Space #1
Space #2
Scale: 1 square = 1 foot on each side

1. How many feet is the perimeter (the distance around the outside) of Space #1?

2. How many feet is the perimeter of Space #2?

3. What is the total perimeter in feet of the entire search region?

4. What is the **area** in square feet of Space #1? (Remember: To calculate area, multiply the length by the width.)

5. What is the area in square feet of Space #2?

6. What is the total area in square feet of the entire search region?

Cracking Secret Codes

Have you ever written a secret message to a friend? Maybe you made up a code that only the two of you knew. Sometimes spies or criminals use secret codes to send messages to one another, and crime fighters need to crack these codes in order to prevent or solve a crime.

What Is a Cryptographer?

A **cryptographer** uses knowledge of mathematics and uses computers to crack codes and learn the meaning of secret messages. Sometimes cryptographers also create codes that are

A cryptographer shows how a secret code can be used to protect information about bank accounts.

then used by people in the government and by crime-fighting groups to keep their own messages to each other secret.

To break a code, cryptographers try to figure out what system was used to create the message. Codes may involve letters of the alphabet, numbers, or a combination of both. Sometimes the coded message will be a series of number, and each number stands for a certain letter of the alphabet. If the cryptographer can figure out which number stands for which letter, then the message can be read.

You Do the Math

Breaking the Code

Here's a code for you to break. In this code, each letter is represented by a certain number. Find the value of each expression to learn the number that stands for each letter. Then, match the letters to the answers under the lines below to see the message.

A: $27 - (9 + 5)$ **C:** $(2 \times 3) + 3$ **D:** $30 - (6 + 6)$ **E:** $(27 + 7) - 30$
F: $(7 \times 7) - 9$ **G:** $(31 - 10) - 5$ **H:** $(6 \times 8) - 4$ **I:** $18 - (1 \times 3)$
M: $79 - (68 - 6)$ **O:** $(3 \times 7) + (9 - 4)$ **R:** $(4 + 20) + 4$
S: $(11 \times 5) - (9 + 3)$ **T:** $90 - (75 + 1)$ **U:** $30 - (2 \times 6)$

$\underline{\quad}$ $\underline{\quad}$ $\underline{\quad}$ $\underline{\quad}$ $\underline{\quad}$ $\underline{\quad}$ $\underline{\quad}$ $\underline{\quad}$ $\underline{\quad}$ $\underline{\quad}$ $\underline{\quad}$ $\underline{\quad}$ $\underline{\quad}$ $\underline{\quad}$ $\underline{\quad}$ $\underline{\quad}$ $\underline{\quad}$

17 13 14 44   15 43   24 43 4 18   14 26   40 15 16 44 14

$\underline{\quad}$ $\underline{\quad}$ $\underline{\quad}$ $\underline{\quad}$ $\underline{\quad}$ $\underline{\quad}$

9   28 15 17   4   43

Fingerprints

If you looked at your fingertips using a magnifying glass, you would see a pattern of ridges and valleys. This pattern is called your fingerprints, and it is yours alone. No two people have the same fingerprints. That is why crime fighters look for fingerprints to help in their investigation.

If fingerprints are found at a crime scene, it proves that the person who made the prints was at the scene. Crime fighters compare prints they find at a crime scene with prints that they have on file or with prints that they take from suspects. You can take someone's fingerprints by putting ink on the person's fingers and then pressing the fingers on a white card. Sometimes print comparison is done by trained investigators who can recognize the differences in people's fingerprints.

Each person's fingerprints are different from every other person's prints.

Fingerprint Scanners

Another way to take fingerprints is with a finger-print scanner. Someone being fingerprinted with a scanner puts each finger, in turn, on a glass plate, and a special camera makes a digital picture of the fingerprint. These machines are also able to compare two sets of fingerprints to see if they are the same.

Fingerprint Patterns

There are 3 main types of fingerprint patterns. *Arches* look like hills, *whorls* look like circles or spirals, and *loops* have long curves. A finger-print expert has created a table showing how often each type of fingerprint pattern was seen in a group of suspects. Each X represents one time. Use the table to answer these questions.

1. How often was the loop pattern seen?
2. Which pattern was seen most often?
3. Which pattern was seen least often?

Frequency of Fingerprint Patterns	
Fingerprint Type	**How Often Each Was Seen**
whorl	x x x x x x x x x
loop	x x x x x x x
arch	x x x x

Arson Alert!

Every year, there are almost 2 million fires in the United States. Most of these fires start by accident, such as wildfires started by lightning. However, about 1 in every 4 fires is set on purpose. Setting a fire on purpose is a crime. The crime is called arson. Arson fires cause billions of dollars worth of damage in the United States each year.

Finding Patterns

Fire investigators who suspect arson look for important clues that may be left in the ashes after a fire has been put out. Sometimes they use specially trained dogs to help them look for clues. The dogs are able to smell substances that are used to set fires.

Investigators look for clues at the scene of a fire they think may have been caused by arson

Investigators pinpoint the locations of arson fires on a map. Looking at the information on the map helps them see patterns in where the fires are occurring. Knowing these patterns may help them predict where a person starting fires will strike next—and help them catch the criminal.

Arson Fires

Fire investigators keep records on how many arson fires are set each year in the United States. This **pictograph** has information about fires that were set in buildings. Use the pictograph to answer the questions.

Arson Fires in Buildings, 2002–2007

Source: United States Fire Administration; data rounded and simplified for pictograph.

Key: 1 house = 3,000 fires

1. What year had the greatest number of arson fires in buildings?
2. How many fewer fires were set in 2007 than in 2003?
3. How many more fires were set in 2007 than in 2006?

If You Want to Be a Crime Fighter

If you would like to work as a crime fighter, there are many different careers that might interest you, including local police officer or state trooper. Some people become specialists, such as fingerprint examiners and handwriting analysts. There are also crime fighters, such as crime scene investigators, who have skills in a wide area.

Solving crimes is almost always a team effort, so you need to be able to work well with other people. It is important to take different types of math classes and to be able to use computers. Computers are an important tool crime fighters use.

To become a police officer, you must graduate from high school. Some police departments require 1 or 2 years of college or perhaps even a 4-year college degree. You must attend a police academy for further training. Many other crime-fighting careers require a 4-year college degree in math or science. Some crime technician careers require a technical certificate, which you can get in 2 years.

Answer Key

Pages 4-5: Using Math to Fight Crime:
1. 16. **2.** computer virus. **3.** 8 times (23 – 15 = 8).
4. 138 (84 + 16 + 23 + 15 = 138).

Pages 6-7: CSI: Crime Scene Investigation:
1. (1, B). **2.** (6, C). **3.** the knight statue. **4.** (3, F).

Pages 8-9: Are You Telling the Truth?:
The ranking from most accurate to least accurate is: Examiner B: $\frac{8}{10}$; Examiner A: $\frac{6}{10}$; Examiner C: $\frac{5}{10}$; Examiner D: $\frac{4}{10}$. Examiner B is the most accurate.

Pages 10-11: Tracking a Criminal: Shoeprints:
Shoeprint 1: Suspect D. Shoeprint 2: Suspect A. Shoeprint 3: Suspect B. Shoeprint 4: Suspect C.

Pages 12-13: Evidence in Writing:
1. Credit card forgery (67). **2.** 7 (19 – 12 = 7).
3. 86 (67 + 19 = 86).

Pages 14-15: Slow Down!:
Driver A traveled 70 miles (125 – 55 = 70); Driver B traveled 54 miles (91 – 37 = 54); Driver C traveled 49 miles (65 – 16 = 49); Driver D traveled 60 miles (109 – 49 = 60). Drivers A and D were speeding. They traveled more than 55 miles in one hour. Drivers B and C were not speeding.

Pages 16-17: Tracking Graffiti:
Each year Maplewood spends $78,000 (30,000 x $2.60 = $78,000), Sycamore spends $56,250 (45,000 x $1.25 = $56,250), and Elmhurst spends $75,000 (75,000 x $1.00 = $75,000). Maplewood spends the most. No, the town with the largest number of people, Elmhurst, does not spend the most.

Pages 18-19: Is This Painting the Real Thing?:
1. 174 (127 + 47 = 174). **2.** 31 (59 – 28 = 31).
3. 121 (78 + 43 = 121).

Pages 20-21: Diving for Evidence:
1. 24 feet (7 + 7 + 5 + 5 = 24). **2.** 12 feet (3 + 3 + 3 + 3 = 12). **3.** The total perimeter is 30 feet (7 + 3 + 3 + 3 + 2 + 7 + 5 = 30). **4.** 35 square feet (7 x 5 = 35). **5.** 9 square feet (3 x 3 = 9). **6.** The total area is 44 square feet (35 + 9 = 44).

Pages 22-23: Cracking Secret Codes:
MATH IS USED TO FIGHT CRIMES. (A = 13; C = 9; D = 18; E = 4; F = 40; G = 16; H = 44; I = 15; M = 17; O = 26; R = 28; S = 43; T = 14; U = 24.)

Pages 24-25: Fingerprints:
1. 7 times. **2.** whorl pattern. **3.** arch pattern.

Pages 26-27: Arson Alert!:
1. 2002. **2.** 6,000 fewer. **3.** 3,000.

Glossary

accurate—Correct.

area—The number of square units needed to cover a surface.

authentic—Not fake.

calculate—To figure out the exact answer to a problem.

cast—An impression formed by pressing soft material over or inside something and letting it harden.

cryptographer—Someone who breaks or creates codes.

difference—The amount by which one number is greater than another number.

digitally scan—To take a picture of something that goes directly into a computer.

estimate—To figure out about how many or how much.

forged—Fake; a forged painting is an illegal copy of a valuable original painting or a painting done in the style of a famous artist to make people think it was created by the famous artist.

graffiti—Words or drawings that are written or painted without permission on walls or other surfaces in public places.

investigator—A person who examines a thing, place, or situation very carefully in order to get information.

mathematician—A person who is an expert about math or who uses math in his or her job.

perimeter—The distance around a figure.

pictograph—A graph that uses symbols to show and compare information.

predict—To make a reasonable guess about what will happen.

sonar—A system for detecting and finding underwater objects.

survey—To ask a group of people a question to gather information.

vandals—People who damage or destroy property.

To Learn More

Read these books:

Fridell, Ron. *Forensic Science*. Minneapolis, Minn.: Lerner Publications, 2007.

Harris, Elizabeth Snoke. *Crime Scene Science Fair Projects*. New York: Sterling Publishing, 2006.

Horn, Geoffrey M. *Crime Scene Investigator*. Pleasantville, N.Y.: Gareth Stevens, 2008.

Teitelbaum, Michael. *Batman's Guide to Crime and Detection*. New York: DK Publishing, 2003.

Look up these Web sites:

Federal Bureau of Investigation (FBI)—Kids' Page
http://www.fbi.gov/fbikids.htm

National Security Agency (NSA): CryptoKids—America's Future Codemakers and Codebreakers
http://www.nsa.gov/kids

Police and Detectives—Career Information
http://www.bls.gov/oco/ocos160.htm

Key Internet search terms:

crime scene investigator, FBI, police detective

Index

About the Author

Sheri L. Arroyo has a master of arts degree in education. She has been an elementary school teacher in San Diego, California, for more than twenty years and has taught third grade for the past thirteen years.